# Spiritual Counsels on the Monastic Life

Starets Barsanuphius of Optina

By Starets Nikona



*Front cover is of unknown Great Schema monks.

## I. The beginning of the monastic life

1. Hieromonk Nikona was the last igumen (abbot) of Optina. The name he was known by in the world was Nicholas Mitrofanovich Belyaev. He was born on September 26th, 1888 to very devout parents. In fact, they had a special relationship with the blessed priest, Saint John of Kronstadt, who visited the family on a regular basis.

Nicholas Belyaev was a very naughty child. However, when he was 16 years old, the death of a relative helped him realise the futility of this world and he decided to become a monk. The very wise archpriest, metropolitan Tryphon Turkestanov, who was a family friend, provided guidance in this decision. Most of Nicholas Belyaev's relatives reacted to his decision with distrust (because of his past mischief) and a fair bit of enmity (they wanted nothing to hear nothing of monasteries). But not everyone. When an acquaintance heard about his decision, she said to him:
-I heard you're going to the monastery. How blessed you are!

2. At the age of 19, Nicholas Belyaev left the world and went to Optina with his brother Ivan, following metropolitan Tryphon Turkestanov's suggestion. The novices were accompanied to the monastery by their pious mother, a spiritual daughter of Saint John of Kronstadt.
When the two lads entered the courtyard of Optina, a monk asked them:
- What do you seek here?

Nicholas replied:
- God's truth.

3. At Optina the two brothers sought out starets Barsanuphius. Metropolitan Tryphon had told them:

- Starets Barsanuphius shall be your spiritual father and elder. However, you need to know that there is a group of monks in Optina, who don't like him at all. They are increasingly turning against him. If anyone speaks badly of the elder to you, do not listen to them!

4. Starets Barsanuphius joyfully welcomed the two lads, who had been referred to him by his good friend, Metropolitan Tryphon. He blessed them and said:

-Thank you, oh Lord, "that you have hidden these things from the wise and understanding and revealed them to little children. Thank you, for leading your servants, John and Nicholas, here.
Grant that they may go through the novitiate with courage, bravery and patience.

(And giving them each a prayer rope, he added:)

This is your weapon. Use it to relentlessly fight your invisible enemies.

Always fear God. You will achieve nothing without fearing God. Your new life begins now.

I love your mother so! How did she manage to bring you here, both her children as a sacrifice to God? And wholeheartedly too? You should be grateful to her for her sacrifice. And for her offering to the monastery. Tell her that I have the noblest feelings for her. I would really like to see her. Maybe she comes again in the summer. I'll still be alive then. May God have mercy on her.

How you ought to thank the Lord for guiding you to the monastery! Do not think for a second that you came on your own accord. No-one comes to me, unless my heavenly Father draws them. God gave you the freedom. On your side, this freedom was simply expressed. You just did not object, when He took you by the hand and led you here! The Lord is the one who saves us. We are not saved on our own accord. He, the Merciful, saves us; our willingness is adequate for him to achieve it.
Thank God that he led you to this monastery, to our quiet and serene Skete. Yes, for only by the help of God can anyone tread the hard and narrow road. If the Lord grants that you live here for the next two or three years, you shall come to see the happiness and joy of monastic life.

5. And thus those two young men, aged 19 and 20 years old, are now novices in a monastery with a strict tradition. Plenty of speculation goes round about them.

-What will they do? Will they cope?
-Will they manage to stay for good?

The Elder Barsanuphius replied:
-They will, if they constantly keep God on their mind.

6. In another similar instance, the elder noted:

-The novice, who comes to the monastery with all his heart and sincere motives, will always be filled with joy.

Not many days went by. Upon noticing the virtues of Elder Barsanuphius and the rest of the brothers in the Skete, Nicholas Belyaev told the elder:
-Elder, I can see I have no virtue. Even worse, I see that my willingness is not unwavering. I realise, I do not know what I should do. My conclusion is this: the best thing for me to do is to act obediently in everything. To do what ever you tell me in every instance. Without Your blessing, I shall do nothing.

Then the elder said to him:
-This your decision is very good indeed.

## II. Spiritual studies

1. Spiritual studies are one of the most important aspects of monastic life. Spiritual progress cannot be made without studying spiritual books and without prayer, says Abba Nilus the Ascetic.

A monk doesn't just read in order to gain theoretical knowledge, but for spiritual profit. What then should he study? How many books?

The elder Barsanuphius used to say:
-Nicholas complains that he has too many questions. He says that there are a lot of things he does not understand. He has literally worn me out with his questions. How does that work? Why is that so? Why this?

I say to him:
-Forgive me but I do not have an answer to all your questions.
-Why is that?
-Because both all my disciples and myself have been up since four o'clock in the morning!
He says:
-I hear some people speak very highly of Abba Dorotheus. But I don't understand anything of what he says!
-And you're sad about that? Do you really not understand anything? But of course you do understand something! God's grace gives to one ten talents and to another a single denarius. But even for that single one, we should thank Him. It is good. When the elder Macarius was a disciple, he was of the opinion that he understood father Dorotheus well. Later, as an hieromonk, he would tell us that there was a lot he didn't understand! If therefore, father Macarius, an angelic mind, did not comprehend this book very well, don't be surprised that you lack in understanding of it. This book is the foundation of monastic life. That's how deep it is! And it has such depth, because it was written by the Holy Spirit. It is no coincidence, that for 15 centuries it has been so highly valued and renowned. And not only for us orthodox Christians but also in the West, in their monasteries.

-But why do I feel no consolation by your words at this time?

-I do not know. It's a hardship. And for this hardship we ought to thank God! His providence knows what is best for us, what is most profitable. But we must

not forget this: we cannot attain everything in a moment -no matter how much integrity we display in our search. A methodical and patient journey is required. Otherwise, we only gather empty knowledge. Nothing more.
And the Elder added:
In Optina, the first book everyone reads is: The Ascetic Words of Abba Dorotheus. Every monk ought to read it from start to finish, at least once every three years. It is the alphabet book of monastic life. New and deeper meanings are revealed every time.

2. The Elder said:
-Make the most of the opportunities you have to study. Do not listen to our enemy, who tells you that you'll have plenty of time in the future and that you will study then. The best time for you further your education is now. Study as much as you can. Fill your mind with plenty of knowledge and your heart with deep humility, regarding yourselves as the least of all. There will come a time when you will no longer be able to study books. Remember my words.
-Father, why do you say we will not be able to study?
-Because in 5-6 years from now you will have moved on to study the book of life.

3. For as long as I live, we shall live together. When I die, I will entrust you to the Lord. I will leave you to God, in the words of the ancient fathers to their disciples.
When it comes to reading, there are no special instructions, but one general principle: First we should read the books that teach actions and then the ones that explain the theory. The Lord will reveal this

to you and you will come to realise, that this principle is correct.

4. Starets Barsanuphius was once tasked with putting together a list of books, deemed appropriate for spiritual study by the monks of Optina. Starets Barsanuphius purposefully left a book of an Agiorite saint off the list, with these words:

Forgive me, saint, for not including your book on the list. But I really don't want the monks, who have found a haven of salvation in Russian monasteries, to be so charmed by what you write, that they all want to leave for Mount Athos!

**III. On music**

1. Starets Barsanuphius had received a substantial education in music. He was actually a great musician. However, when he became a monk, he also studied the futility of music. And he said:
Music distracts man's thoughts and attention from the words and focuses them on the melody, thus obstructing prayer. This is why music does not profit even those who sing! If they sing well, they become vain. If they sing badly, they are filled with disappointment and bitterness. The psalter is extremely restricted by the notes, they bind him. The freedom of creativity, feelings and prayer ceases to exist. The soul remains silent. And sweet sounds are the only thing to be heard! With no meaning. No content. Words lose their significance. No-one pays attention to them anymore. And no-one prays.

2. A visitor asked the Elder.
-Are there any nightingales around here?

He replied:
-I don't know. I'm not looking out for their singing. But there are certainly wolves. And they sing in unison, like a choir. Just like European music choirs.

## IV. His tonsure

1. On April 16th 1909, Good Friday that year, took place the novices' tonsure to rasophora. Amongst them was Nicholas Belyaev, who was given the name Nikona at that point.
2.
Following the tonsure, the new monks proceeded to visit and worship the graves of the holy Elders and asked for their blessing. Next, they visited starets Barsanuphius, who happened to be ill and bedridden, in order to receive his blessing.

The Elder told them:
-God's special blessing is at work in you now. Right now begins for you this new life. The direction a monk takes straight after his tonsure, stays with him till the grave. You have now become monks, rasophoras. It's not like taking office in a worldly sense. On the monastic habit are written these words: If anyone amongst you would be first, he must be servant of all. Be humble. Be as humble as you can. God's grace will now be of more comfort to you than before; the enemy also will now fight you much more. Therefore, I warn you: be prepared for sorrows and temptations.

2. The Elder said:
- You became a monk the very moment you received the Despot's blessing! The Despot -given he has a sense of humour- may have even said it in jest! But a high priest's words always have tremendous power. The high priestly blessing is no small matter. The Despot may very well be a sinner, like all people. And yet, both his blessing and his prayers have great power.

## V. The spiritual relationship of Elder and disciple

1. Starets Barsanuphius said:
In the old times, the relationship between an abba (father) and his disciples was characteristically defined by simplicity. The abba used to be a true father; neither a master nor a leader, to whom they had to submit! This simplicity was also omnipresent in our Skete at the time of our great elders. Later on however, after starets Anatolius' death, it started to diminish. Some people now tell me that I overdo it in my simplicity towards the brothers. I cannot act in a different manner. If some people take advantage of this simplicity of mine, that cannot allow me to have cold and formal relationships with everyone, just because of them! I had a conversation on this exact topic today: that I act in an overly straight-forward and simple manner. A holy father had received similar complaints. He replied to them:

"You wish me to leave behind this simplicity? For thirty years I have toiled to gain it! And you now tell me to leave it in a single moment?"

2. At one point, father Nikona was bogged down with a lot of thoughts.
-What's going on with you? the Elder asked.
-It's on my mind that I have been given a lot, and therefore a lot will be asked of me.
The Elder replied:
-You're in a very privileged position. You constantly have an elder by your side. You can tell him anything you like. I never had that privilege. Especially after the death of starets Anatolius! Perhaps sometime you also will experience this deprivation! Then you will understand!

And the Elder continued:
-I cannot get rid of the thought, that I have done very little for my spiritual children and have not taken enough care of them. As long as I live and am in this position, you will live in peace. In a decade's time, you will have to stand on your own, on your two feet. But I don't think I'll be alive at that point! You will suffer after my death, you will end up on your own! Then you will step into my shoes. You will feel exactly the same way I felt after father Anatolius' death. Everything will depend on you alone. So while there is still time, save up on patience now! Don't be shaken, I have this thought all the time nowadays; that very soon I will die. And when I have been placed in the dark soil, keep visiting my grave and praying for for my soul and say: "The elder truly loved me"!
And having said those words, father Barsanuphius hugged father Nikona tightly and kissed him.

3. When I have been buried in the dark soil, then you will be orphaned; then you will be orphaned.

4. The starets Barsanuphius used to say:
Our whole life is a mystery, only known to God! Nothing in life classifies as an accident. There are no coincidences. Everything is mapped out by God's Providence. We often fail to understand the significance of various incidents. It feels like we have a lot of boxes before us, but no keys! Pay attention to what happens in your life, in different instances. Everything holds a very deep meaning, a lot of which might be incomprehensible at present. It will be revealed to you gradually in the future.

5. I wish to live for a bit longer. To help you stand firm, not only in your spiritual life but also your external one: to make you a rasophora. In addition, I would like to be there in time to make you a stavrophora. But alas, I know not! Will I be alive, I wonder? When you come a stavrophora, you will be given the seal of our King! Whether you then keep it or rub it off, will be dependant on you! While I am still alive, make every effort to be strengthened! What will happen after that, I do not know.

6. Father Nikona asked:
- Why do present-day monastics not have the same virtues as monks of the past?

The Elder answered:
-A spiritually weak world will produce weak monastics.

Once, when father Nikona's soul was plagued with thoughts of reproach and accusation, the Elder took his head between his hands and looking him in the eye, said:
-Above and before everything else, comes humility! Be humble! Be humble!

7. The Elder said:
-You can choose from different types of wood, in order to light a fire; yew logs, pine log. The important thing is for the house to get warm.

His aim was to emphasize that prayer is valuable in of itself, no matter how it is uttered; the way it is said, is not as important.

The elder said:
-You Nicholas, have a very strong will. I feel like we should walk this road of monastic life together, helping each other along the way. A monk is like a broken roof-tile. Everyone hits it. Demons. Humans. He expects to receive humiliation from everyone. They hit him so much, that he ends up like the fine red soil, from which the tile was made in the first place! But the Lord takes him and turns him into steel. Only he won't become steel in this life, but there! (And he pointed to heaven).

## VI. Signs of the end

1. In 1909, at the age of 64, the starets said:
- I am starting to feel helpless. I cannot do anything anymore. It feels like my days are now numbered. One thing I ask of God. That you may stand strong on

your two feet. You are about to embark on military service. Yes. You are. You will “serve in the army”. You will then acquire a better understanding of what hides beneath the sheepskin, by which this beast -the world- often introduces itself to us in. Because sometimes it seems pleasant. Full of beautiful flowers. And everyone rushes to enjoy its beauty. Then the beast-world removes its mask and devours them. Do not be misguided by these deceitful things. Keep in mind, that the only sheep-related thing here is the skin; nothing else.

2. In 1909 he began to speak of his death; that it was close at hand; that its first indications were there: pain in the legs.

-These are forebodings of the end; it is near. I cannot hold on for any longer. I can barely sit up sometimes. How would I walk?! And yet I wish to live for a bit longer, even if in such a state. Death is formidable! I am filled with terror at the thought of being called to answer for my spiritual children.

In April 1909, while father Nikona was by his side, father Alexius brought the elder Barsanuphius a package, sent by a nun. He opened it and found the great angelic schema (image).

After father Alexius had left, he said:

“It has been my deep longing, to receive the great angelic schema, before my death. I hadn’t confided in anyone about it, apart from the archimandrite and general abbot of Optina. I have now received it. I perceive this as an sign of my death! It is close by. This is my final wish and I pray it comes true. I hope to die soon after its fulfilment, in a few hours!”

## VII. The hardship of obedience

1. In March 1912, starets Barsanuphius could barely stand on his feet during the service on the Fifth Sunday of Lent. He felt so poorly, that he had to leave halfway through. He went to his cell and lay down, unable to stand.
When his disciple visited him after the liturgy, he asked:
-What did the Gospel say today?

He replied:
-See, we are going up to Jerusalem, and the Son of Man will be delivered over, and they will mock Him and flog Him, and spit on Him and kill Hi,

Then the Elder said:
-These are the stages of the ascent to the Jerusalem above! We also must go through them! I wonder which stage we are at now?

2. Many envied him because of his virtues, for they did not have them and could not mimic them.

Different groups had started to form in Optina. The group of starets Joseph did not love starets Barsanuphius at all. There was underlying jealousy in the air. Starets Barsanuphius was highly educated, originated from a prestigious Orenburg family, musical, had been a highest ranking officer in the army and came to Optina as a priest. On the other hand, Starets Joseph stood out purely for his vast humility and kindness. So when the blessed elder Joseph fell asleep in the Lord, the jealousy, now unbridled, showed its face. The accusation was brought forth. And the Synod's decision arrived, aiming to pacify the situation in the Monastery: starets Barsanuphius is to be ordained as archimandrite and appointed as abbot at the Staro Golutvin Monastery, near Moscow.

When the Elder was informed of the decision, he bowed his head and completely crushed, whispered: "See, we are going up to Jerusalem".

Upon seeing his immense sorrow, the brothers at the Monastery suggested he raise health reasons -he was in an awful state anyway- and refuse to leave his "repentance".

The Elder refused to accept this way out, commenting, "The apostle said: be an example to the faithful."

And he became a model of obedience.

On the 2nd of April 1912, the Monday of Thomas, with tears in his eyes and his soul brimming with grief and bitterness, he left, yearning for a "faraway land".

-I am so sad, he said, that I fear I will lose my mind!

This is how he experienced the "promotion"! And how vast and endless his obedience!

At Golutvin the Elder suffered constantly. Psychologically, due to the sorrow of his removal from his beloved Optina. And physically, because the

cancer plaguing him. Such was his pain, physical and of the soul, that he experienced the mystery of our Lord's crucifixion. To the doctors, who went to offer some alleviation, he would say:
-Leave me alone. I am on the cross.

In such a state and realising that he had nothing to offer at the monastery of Golutvin through his obedience anymore, he asked for a request to the Synod to be prepared, in order that he may be relieved from his duties as an abbot and be allowed to return to Optina. As soon as he signed it, he joyfully exclaimed:
-As soon as I receive approval, I will leave for Optina straight away. I want to leave my bones there!

But it wasn't to be. In the early morning of April 1st 1913, he gave his pure soul up to the Lord, whom he had so loved and for who's sake he had increasingly crucified himself until his final moment.
His relic was brought to Optina immediately to be buried, after being absent for exactly 365 days.

## VIII. Handkerchiefs for the tears of endurance

1. Upon receiving the order to move out of Optina, the Elder Barsanuphius gave his disciple, father Nikona, two small handkerchiefs, as a gift to be remembered by.

The young monk looked at them with sadness and whispered under his breath:

-Handkerchiefs. Handkerchiefs. What else could they be for, but to wipe my tears, when the great sorrow comes, as he has foretold me.

2. As they said their goodbyes and he left his favourite disciple behind, he blessed him and said:
-Lord, save your servant Nikona. Become his helper and protector. And give him strength, when he no longer has family or a place to hide!

The Elder had prophesied. And father Nikona, who by now was accustomed to hearing about the future, understood! He bowed down before the Elder and sobbing violently, he returned to his cell with his eyes full of tears, saying:
- Handkerchiefs. Handkerchiefs. Where are you, for I need to wipe away the first tears?

Will those handkerchiefs of the Elder Barsanuphius suffice for the blessed hieromonk Nikona to wipe his tears of endurance till 1931, throughout a lifetime of continuous ascent, pain and trails, of giving up his soul? All this, so that he may ascend to the Jerusalem Above via the Cross.

## IX. On antichrist

The words of Starets Barsanuphius:
-No-one knows at what time the Antichrist will come. There are plenty of signs, that he will be coming soon. We ought to think that the time is very near indeed, especially when this sort of persecution of the faith increases and they try hard to snuff it out. Nonetheless, nothing can be stated persistently or

with certainty. For there were other times, when they thought he was coming, but they were wrong.

## X. The persecutions of the final days

Thus said Elder Barsanuphius:

-Monastics will face refined trials in the last days. Upon surface-level inspection, one wouldn't really be able to call them trials! Yet this is the cunning work of our enemy. Obvious, cruel and full-on torment induces in the Christian a passionate zeal to endure. The enemy has abandoned obvious torture. He now prefers lower-scale and refined torture, that actually ends up much more effective! These hardships don't incite zeal in one's heart. In contrast, you end up in a state, where you do not know what you should do, in a constant vortex of rumination. They slowly suck up one's strength, exhausting their psychological stamina and leading them to despair, helplessness, indecisiveness. Thus they lead them to ruin. One becomes a dwelling to passions. For they have ended up being weakened and filled with sorrow and disappointment. This is all due to the fact, that monastics of the final days await for better times to contend, as they should. "We will fast and pray, they say, when the circumstances are right"! But the Lord has promised us, that He will forgive us our sins, when we repent; he hasn't promised us, that we would be alive tomorrow. Therefore, we ought to keep our commandments and promises in every circumstance, whether good or bad and never forget these words: "Behold, now is the favourable time; behold, now is the day of salvation".

## XI. The gravestone

On it was written:

Archimandrite Barsanuphius
Born 5th July 1845
Fell asleep 1st April 1913

Rejoice always. Pray without ceasing. Give thanks in all circumstances.
The one who endures to the end, he will be saved.
I waited patiently for the Lord and He inclined to me and heard my cry.

## XII. His confidence before God

Would such a man not have gained such confidence before the Lord? And would he have not expressed it in caring for his favoured disciple, father Nikona?

In 1931, the hieromonk Nikona finds himself exiled in Siberia. He is very ill and everything points towards the end being near. He himself can sense it. And he prays. He asks God to reveal to someone, whether he is going to live for a little longer or die.

And behold, shortly before his death, one of his spiritual daughters had a dream, that shook her with its vividness.

She saw starets Barsanuphius moving father Nikona's belongings, from his cell-lodging to exile in Siberia. She respectfully watches on in silence, but is slightly perplexed. However, when she saw him taking father Nikona's bed at the very end, she could contain herself no longer and spoke up.

-Elder, she said, why are you taking his bed? Where will he sleep now?

The great starets calmly replied:
-Do not worry. He is moving for good. He is coming to be close to me. He no longer needs this bed. I will give him my own.

When the woman, ignorant of what had previously happened, wrote her dream to her spiritual father, father Nikona responded to her thus:
-Your dream seems true. I don't believe in dreams of course. But some dreams come true. It seems that the Lord has decided to take me.

A few days later, the blessed starets Nikona committed his holy soul to the Lord.

His Elder, the great starets Barsanuphius had prepared a place for him and received him in his arms for eternity.

## Spiritual Instructions on Monasticism

### I. On outward conduct

1. Ensure you carry out all you can in an independent manner. Make an effort to not benefit from the labour of others. Do not store any food in your cell. Always be punctual for meals. You may drink up to three cups of tea in your cell, as appointed by the Elders But never visit one another's cells for tea, even if invited. At the table, eat until you are full; but not too full. As time goes on, fasting and abstinence will become absolutely essential to you; optional to an extent. Sleep for six hours at a time; three of them should be uninterrupted sleep. It's absolutely necessary. For a monk, sleep and the stomach are interconnected. One will sleep a lot on a full stomach; more than they should.

2. Go to church and perform your "canon" uninterrupted and without going in and out. Try to start going to church from the very start. Make an effort to get there first. For us here at the Skete, matins is of great importance. On it is founded the whole life of the Skete. It does have a catch though. For those of us, who in the world got used to waking up late, matins is the hardest practice of the monastic life. Therefore, we must cut ourselves no slack, even from our very early days! Forsaking matins and various other weaknesses stem from a lack of determination. Deciding to do what we should, whatever the cost, is of utmost importance. When we

display such determination, God comes to our aid. Did you make the decision to forsake the world? Behold, the Lord helped you. You left the world. The same principle is true in every situation.
When you are asked to do a work of ministry, while performing your canon, go and do it with no indignation. You are being called to do something good. Obedience precedes fasting and prayer.

3. As far as you can, maintain silence. However, if you are asked something -even inside church- reply without fretting or frowning.

4. No-one is to be allowed into your cell, before they say the following blessing: “Through the prayers of our Holy Fathers, Lord Jesus Christ, our God, have mercy and save us”.

5. When you greet someone who belongs to the fellowship, always aim to be the first to bow, even though you may be older than them. And if he is a Hieromonk, ask for his blessing.

6. Now is the time to read books. There will come a time when you will no longer be able to read. The desire to study will be there, but not the time! And for every single time that you had the opportunity, you will later be sad and full of regrets for no reading more. Studying will strengthen your willpower.

**II. About prayer**

1. Hold your three hundred knots rosary strongly in your hands. You should do it accurately and carefully.

Hold it like a palm branch - as a symbol of victory· and you will not be deceived. It has great, mysterious, power.

2. Jesus prayer must be said in its entirety· without condensing it. This consignment was given to us by the holy Elders. And the stress must be highlighted on the last word: the sinner. The purpose of this prayer is always one: the memory of God.

3. Your first task, as soon as you wake up, should be the sign of the honest and life-giving Cross· and your first words, the words of Jesus prayer. When you are able to, make the prayer with the rosary in hand. When you are engaged in a project, then without the rosary.

4. When thoughts come to you, do not try to banish them by opening a rational dialogue with them. Smash them on the stone. The Stone is Christ. His Name. The prayer of Jesus. It is not in your control to banish thoughts. But, it is under your control not to accept them. The thoughts are driven away only by the Name of Jesus.

5. When the prayer - it happens sometimes - is done carelessly and mechanically, do not be disappointed. At the time of prayer in the name of the Lord Jesus Christ even our mouths are sanctified.

6.You should keep Jesus prayer uninterrupted. Lord Jesus Christ, Son of God, have mercy on me, a sinner. And you should reveal your thoughts. All of our holy Fathers say, that it is impossible to continue the Jesus

Prayer without controlling our thoughts. The Name of Jesus abolishes every evil and cunning act. The devil is powerless before the power of the Name of the Lord. And all his traps ending up to dust. Why is this happening? And how is this happening? We do not know. We only know that, this is how it is. Our self-control for the continuance of the Jesus Prayer requires, above all, to reveal our thoughts. And above all, and before all: to have humility, and to show humility.

7. Prayer is external, is said out-loud, and internal, otherwise mental and to the heart. But there is an even higher kind of prayer: the spiritual prayer. Those who have this prayer begin to understand the mysteries of nature, their meaning and content. They see the sensory reality around them from the inside, from the spiritual side of it. That is why they have a different spiritual joy˙ and that is why tears often come to their eyes. To us, their joy is incomprehensible. We understand the joy of artists: of poets, of musicians, of painters, but their joy is comparatively null, because it is mental. Saint Isaac the Syrian is also referring to a fourth kind of prayer, which passes beyond the limits of our own ability to understand it. What prayer is this? I do not know. Maybe only Saint Isaac had this kind of prayer.

8. Saint Seraphim of Sarov says: In the monastery, whoever does not say the Jesus Prayer is not a monk. And he adds something terrible: The one does not say the Jesus Prayer is a burnt torch. Yes, it is of a great need to have a kind of Jesus Prayer. Even the lowest one!

9. The main element in the prayer is patience. The enemy tries in every way to distract the monk's devotion from the Jesus Prayer. The accomplishment lies in the continuance of the Jesus Prayer with patience.

10. The work of bishop Ignatius Brianchaninov is irreplaceable. It is the Alphabet. The work of bishop Theophan the Recluse is the Grammar. It is deeper. Even the advanced ones when they read them they need to put some effort. The Jesus Prayer cannot be learned only by reading! We learn it mainly empirically. The Jesus Prayer is a sea without shore. Impossible to pass through it. Impossible to describe it in books. Many start to do it. Few can reach it. Very few acquire the inner Jesus Prayer. This work has unfortunately been almost forgotten! We don't even talk about it anymore!

11. For the one that has the inner Jesus Prayer, his prayer is so natural, so like his own thing, as it is his breath. Whatever he does, his prayer comes automatically, from within. In the temple, he watches what they sing and what they read, and at the same time he rises at his inside. May the Jesus Prayer bind to your breath. The Prayer does not stop even during sleep time. It takes place in his heart. I am asleep and my heart is awake. We do not have such a situation. We wake up, and we do not find the name of Jesus in our mouths.

12. It is different the characteristic of the beginner' different is the characteristic of the advanced one in the mental work. It is easier to pay attention to the words of the troparions and the texts, than to protect

yourself from the division of meditation. So, make it a rule to pay attention to the troparions and the texts. Sometimes, of course, it is better someone to say the Jesus Prayer than to hear what they are reading and chanting. We need to have some perception.

13. The words of the psalm They completely compassed me, after which it is repeated three times but in the name of the Lord I repulsed them. , (Psalm 117, 10,12) are fully understood by all those who say the Jesus Prayer[1], without having read any interpretation. They understand that they are talking about the prayer of Jesus. And there are many such words in the psalms.

14. Can the one who has reached the inner prayer to lose the Jesus Prayer? I think yes. He can. If he falls into disorder and concerns. Sometimes the Lord takes away the Jesus Prayer from us. His will is inscrutable. This is what happened to the Great Schema Monk Cleopas. For two years he felt, that he had lost his close hearted Jesus Prayer! Then it came back. Maybe the Lord did it to test him. We must never despair.

15. This tedious - often graceless – state, that we have to go through in order to reach the inner Jesus Prayer, is not necessary for everyone. But generally, the order is this: It takes a lot of effort and a lot of sadness and one of them is this graceless state.

---

[1] The Jesus Prayer: "Lord Jesus Christ, Son of God, have mercy on me a sinner".

16. The Lord, the giver of the blessing to the one that asks for it, also gives the inner Jesus Prayer. Sometimes He gives it shortly before death.

17. The first gift of the Lord for the prayer is attention, that is, to keep our minds on the words of the Jesus Prayer, without being abstracted. But when we pray like this, the heart is silent. And here is the issue. Then, to us the thought is not united with the emotions. There is no agreement between them. The second stage of prayer is, when the mind is united with the heart and thus united it ascends to God. Third is the spiritual prayer. I do not know anything and I do not have anything to say about it. The man, who has the spiritual prayer, although he lives on earth, with his mind and heart, that is, with his whole soul, is close to God. Those who have reached this kind of prayer see everything with spiritual eyes˙ and they have both knowledge and sight. You can pray, God to give you the gift to pray carefully. But it is a sin to ask God for the highest levels of prayer. You must leave this entirely at His disposal.

18. Saint John of Kronstadt was a great luminary of Russia. He was a burning and shining lamp! He had the gift of inner prayer to a great extent. His hieratic activity was so great, that we wonder how his body withstood so much effort. I remember the words of the apostle: My strength is manifested in its fullness when I am in this weakness. It is noticed, that men with a great spiritual life leave this world in the memory day of the saint, who was almost in the same struggle like them or had the same gift as them. Father John felt asleep in the memory of Saint

Hieromartyr Ignatius the Theophorus (God-Bearer), the primogenitor of the Jesus inner prayer.

19. I was engaged with the Jesus Prayer. The service was progressing well. The Prayer started to warm me up. But my promotion to abbot, erased it. Now my prayer is hardly breathing! I often wonder: Do I win with this benefice or do I lose?

20. Some people imagined that I was enchanted! When I lived with vigilance and prayer, I was engaged with the Jesus Prayer. Now they tell me: Either you pray -or you do not pray, it is the same thing. You are not going to prosper in prayer. Those times are over. But this is a thought, brought to me by the devil. Because the Jesus prayer is necessary for us, to enter the kingdom of heaven.

21. For a long time I could not understand, what is the union of the mind with the heart. It is the union of the forces of the soul into one. And it is accomplished when they all turn to God, so that their division is impossible. What beauty does a note or a sound have when we have them individually or out of their position? None. But these same sounds in the hands of genius composers acquire great power and beauty. Jesus prayer has no limits. It is such kind of a bond, that no matter how much you unbind it, it always stays a bond. The mind, when is practicing in the study of the Scriptures and in prayer, is enlightened. While when it sinks to the earthly material, it becomes heavy and incapable of understanding the spiritual things. It is as necessary to study books spiritually as it is to strive to overcome the passions. We overcome the passions easily, when they are just

in the mind. But when they cross over into words or deeds, they become rooted. And then uprooting them is very difficult, if not impossible. The whole life of a monk is a struggle with his thoughts. And that is why Jesus prayer is needed. Whoever does not unite with the Lord Jesus here, he will never unite with him, says Symeon the New Theologian. Devastatingly sound words! When, I was still a submissive, and I read them, I sought a confirmation of them, because these words are only said by Saint Symeon. Then I remembered the words of the Gospel, blessed are the ones that are pure in heart, that they see God, that when we change the order of the words, we have, God is seen by the ones that are pure in heart. But pure heart is the inner prayer of Jesus, the union of mind and heart, to turn together to God.

22. The Prayer in our own words is allowed only outside the Church. During the sacred services we say the intercessory prayer. At that time, we are not allowed to pray in our own words. We must pay attention to what they read. The Jesus prayer - during the sacred services- can only be said during occasional breaks, and when it happens that, we should not listen to what they are reading or chanting.

23. You should seek the spirit. The spirit vitalizes. The letter kills.

24. Whose saint the memory do we have today? Do we have the memory of Saint Maximus the Confessor? Yes. Have you noticed the saint's kontakion? No. Bring the Menaion. Read. The luminous light entered your soul, you were chosen as a vessel, you of the blessed memory. Here is referred

to the Jesus prayer. And below, teaching inaccessible meanings, blissful one, that you are beyond everything˙ and preach the Trinitarian God, that is clearly preexisting and before the beginning of the world. Now I understand, why the elder Ambrosios always had a book of Saint Maximos in his hand. His works are truly deep and truly spiritual.

25. It is a great thing to pray to the great ascetics, the ones known for their holiness. They do not need our prayers as much as we do need theirs. When we remember them, we are the ones to benefit from that action. Because then, they remember us and advocate for us.

26. You have surely noticed, that at the end of my night prayers I mention many saints. Do not think that it is done by chance, or for no reason. An event of my life is connected with the name of every saint I mention. I never forget their names. I have noticed that in this way I have escaped from dangers and generally unpleasant situations.

27. The psalm of He who dwells in the shelter of the Most High must be known by heart.

28. The devil will not let you take a single step of spiritual prosperity, without fighting hard. For every step you make you will fight. In this war only one is our weapon – the Jesus prayer. The saints have said: With this weapon you should strike the invisible enemies˙ there is no greater or stronger weapon either on earth or in heaven. Just thinking about these words – they sound tremendously great- one can realize that there is no more powerful weapon in heaven! And in

the name of Jesus, everyone from the heavens and the earth and the depths will bend ˙ and every tongue will confess, that Lord is Jesus Christ. What mighty times will come to us.

## III. About the monastic life

1. The monastic life should advance gradually. This is the science of all the science. In order someone to study any science, he needs a guide with experience on it. Thus, in order to move forward in a monastic life, one needs to remain faithful to his Elder. However, since it is possible for a spiritual separation to occur, it is worthy asking [ how will it ever be possible for it not to occur].

2. There are two types of a monastic state: The external and the internal. The external one, that of the monastic skouphos[2], is easily found, as Saint John Climacus says. It is easy to become a monk from the outside˙ difficult to become a monk from within. A monk from within one can be even inside the world˙ but this does not mean that one really finds such monks in the world. Nowadays it is very rare to talk about a monk from within. More or less people do not understand this term either. A monk on the outside is the one who is engaged in external works: fasting, vigil, external typical attendance of the sacred services and sobriety. It is not possible for anyone to overtake this status of a monk outside˙ but neither is one allowed to cling to them. External works alone, without internal ones, will cause damage. External

---

[2] A monastic head covering for men. Similar to a beanie.

works can be paralleled with the digging of the earth. No matter how hard you dig, nothing will grow unless you sow. The interior works are the sowing. The wheat is the prayer of the heart. The Jesus Prayer sanctifies the whole inner life of the monk. It gives him strength for the war. The inner monastic life is its cleansing from the passions, the war against the thoughts. We especially need the Jesus prayer, when we are going through trials and tribulations. Firstly, one will find the external monk, that is, the monk of the formalities˙ but one must not dwell on that. He has to go further. The monastic state is more than just an inner cassock, the boiling water and the rice. Of course, we have to wear the monastic clothes and fast˙ but that is not enough. The outside acts alone do not avail. It also needs a fire˙ from within. Monk is the hidden man of the heart, said Staretz Anatoly. When one throws the weight on the formalities, then it is very difficult for him to stay in the monastery! There are many ordinary monks. But there are others, only few, who are ignited by the love of God and worship Him in spirit and in truth. These are the most genuine idealists. Such men God wants, such men He calls close to Him.

3. Only he who thanks God for His mercy to remove him from the world and lead him to the monastery feels good inside the monastery. And on the contrary, he who grumbles about his life in the monastery, inside the monastery he feels really bad. The whole life of the monk is from within, since all the work of the monk is an internal work. Externally, such as temperance and exercise, is just a method. If man, and especially the monk, observes his life, he will see that his whole life is a constant miracle. Penetrating into

the inner meaning we see an amazing wisdom in everything, a scarcely visible depth. Saint John Climacus says: the light of the monks is the angels. The light of the world is the monks. Do not forget, that we must be the light of the world. And our destiny is, in the future life to become kings and priests.

4. The mantle and the schema are of a great importance. They declare, that to the one who wears them was given the grace to live monastically· to complete the monastic promises. The middle of the monastic path is very difficult. It is the most difficult point of the whole monastic path. At the beginning of the road, the grace of the Lord helps and comforts us. In the middle there is the biggest heatwave.

5. You came here to seek God. Everyone is looking for God. Our goal is to find God. It is possible that someone will live in the monastery and never find anything! and never become a true monk! Everyone is looking for God. And the artists· especially the poets· and the painters· and especially the musicians. But they do not seek God like that! How do they seek Him? By keeping the commandments of God. In Pushkin's poem, the Prophet, there are the words:
The angelic fluttering up and the motion of the unknown animals to us at the bottom of the sea below. To us, these two movements (up and down!) go in parallel! But we must try to think only of the above ones. No one can do that at first, but little by little. It needs patience. And then the down movement becomes more and more calm. And maybe we get to the point where only the upper one is left.

6. It is not strange at all that monks also have weaknesses. Monks are people too. So, when a person comes to the monastery, he does not immediately become apathetic. His passions and weaknesses still exist. The difference is that: In the world man did not fight against them˙ while here, in the monastery, even if he is defeated, he never stops fighting. Remain monks until the end of your life. The joy of the monk must be his humility˙ his humility and his simplicity.

7. Staretz Ambrosio was once asked: What is the monastic state? The elder answered: A blissfully state. And indeed. Monastic life is so blissfully that it is impossible for a man to even imagine a happier state of life on earth. But the monastic state is neither as easy as some people imagine, nor as difficult as others think. When I was still a cosmic man I wrote a poem dedicated to Staretz Ambrosios: Lucky he, who walks the narrow street. I printed it in Kazan and sent it to the Elder. Later, when I went to Optina, I found the Elder and reminded him of the poem. The Elder then said to me:
-Ah, so you have it close to you? And he showed me my chest. I mechanically felt the pocket of my shirt, on my chest. And I said:
-No.- Hm ... No ... And how so? I did not understand anything at all. But, as I was told, Elder Ambrosios never said unnecessary words not even for a joke. So, I went and asked his subordinates, Fr. Ilarion and Fr. Ionas, each one separately. They both gave me the same explanation: - Close to you, means in your heart. That is, the Elder asked you: do you live it? do you fulfill it? do you respond to the mental state, that you describe? Then, I understood what he told me. I realized that I did not have the poem with me! But

Elder Ambrose had it with him. Very close to him.

8. If those who want to go to a monastery knew, what bitterness awaits them there, no one would go to the monastery. But the Lord hides these sorrows from us. And if people knew, what happiness and bliss awaits the monks, the whole world would go to the monasteries. The essence of monastic life is the struggle against our passions. The monastic life should never go on by its own volition. The monk must look like an angel. What is a monk? A man who obeys all the commandments of God.

9. The monk, who endures all in good faith, will receive a crown of martyrdom. Humility and love are the greatest virtues. And they must be the significantly characteristics of the monk.

10. Do not think, that you can fly in the sky at once! You cannot. You must first endure sorrows, humiliations and wickedness˙ both within you, from the devil˙ and on the outside, from the unprosperous of the brotherhood. In the beginning we have to go through many temptations. Because we have to understand, what war against passions means and to get a humble idea of ourselves˙ and then, sometimes you will feel hatred and disgust for the monastic life. You have to carry through this all.

11. Our modern monks want to do their will in everything! But Abbot Dorotheus says: I do not think there is another fall for the monk, worse, than to follow his will! The monastic life got out of her way. And yet, even in our time, the devil does not like monasticism, since he fights it with so much fury.

Because the world is held by the monks. When the monks cease to exist, the coming Judgment will come.

## IV. On obedience

The way of obedience is the best and shortest way. Obedience transcends natural human powers. This is why the Lord provides the strength necessary for its observance. When a disciple begins the task of obedience, the Lords strengthens him. He takes this strength as from the Lord's hand. As an affirmation, that obedience is His will.

2. One can state that obedience is an unattainable feat, as a sign of humility; but only when it is actually the case. However, it is completely unacceptable to persist in this thought.

3. We ought to take on "every obedience" assigned to us, hopeful of God's help.

## V. On humility

1. Humility is the cornerstone of monastic life. Humility and obedience aid us in acquiring all the other virtues. Because where there is pride, everything is lost! A man with substantial virtues but also proud, is like a ship loaded with precious and expensive cargo that sinks at open sea, before arriving into the port! "Who will I look to, but him who is humble and contrite in spirit and trembles at my word?" says the Lord. The monastic world is a great

sea with no shore. You cannot neither exhaust it nor sail right through it. The person who hasn't entered this pathway, cannot understand the 'why', it is the narrow and hard way. You can only tread it with God's help: "For my yoke is easy, and my burden is light". At first glance, these words seem contradictory. On the one hand, we are told this road is easy. On the other side, we are told it is narrow and sorrowful. Indeed, it is narrow and hard only for whoever gets on it begrudgingly, by necessity, through no internal will of their own; for some other reason, not the salvation of their soul. For them it is narrow and difficult. But for those who enter the monastic life with a pure desire and longing to worship God in spirit and truth, it is a light burden.

2. The Elders father Macarius and father Ambrosius, as well as all our other Elders, used to say: "Be humble. Humility is the first thing you should have". They would repeat that phrase all the time. Towards the end of his life Saint John the Theologian would only say: "Little children, love one another". Our elders often said: "Be humble". For those two virtues, love and humility, are as interconnected as light and heat.

3. Never act in pride or vanity. Neither when you are alone nor in the presence of others! Consider yourselves worse than everyone. Get accustomed to the thought that you are condemned; you deserve hell; and you can avoid it only by God's mercy. This is no easy task. Only the saints succeed. They alone considered themselves worthy of hell and worse than everyone else.

4. The more you live in the monastery, the more certainty you gain that the Lord looks to the humble and contrite. Pride is a characteristic of the devil.

5. If humility is present, all is well. If there is no humility, all is lost; even though you could be performing miracles! Display humility! Blessed are the pure in heart. A humble person cannot but be pure in heart. Therefore, the humble "will see God".

6. Abba Dorotheus teaches us to keep close watch of ourselves; to inspect our lives; to think about what we have achieved. Being careful in this manner is very important. As a general rule, progress is rooted in humility. A monk cannot remain stationary. He is either progressing or regressing. Not even for a minute does he stay in the same place. He is always moving.

7. The prophet David said: "The faithful have vanished". Why have they vanished? Because "truth has diminished; everyone utters lies to his neighbour"; because we no longer converse in order to benefit spiritually. Instead we speak nonsense and useless words! The prophet David said: "I was brought low and he saved me" (Psalm 114,6). Humility is sufficient for our salvation. In yet another psalm he says: "Consider my humility and my trouble, and forgive all my sins". These words were uttered by the prophet David, because true humility is always acquired with hardship. The way of humility and forbearance in the face of exhaustion, is a difficult path. Many took it, determined to tread it, but couldn't endure it. The bishop Ignatius Brianchaninov himself proceeded to walk on this road also, but

didn't persist. Although he passed through Optina. Tradition has it, that starets Leon had said: "If he hadn't gone a different way, he would have become a second Arsenius the Great". Though he is considered the teacher of contemporary monasticism (for in order to grasp the essence of monastic life in our day, it is essential to study his works), he did not become like Arsenius the Great. He is a saint; but not an Arsenius.

8. Humble yourselves. Endure all. Train yourselves in humility and patience. And you will have peace in your soul. Whoever has internal peace, feels like he is in paradise, even in prison! Macarius the great says: Everyone, even saints, have some sort of pride. How deep inside us is rooted this vile thing! Only angels are not proud (they are clean!), as well as those who leave this earth and go to heaven.

9. "Self-deprecation is an invisible ascent" says Saint John Climacus. Holding ourselves accountable for our weaknesses is a necessary requirement to be humbled. Nonetheless, we should take care not to end up exhausted and despairing. Whatever happens, we should never lose our courage. In this war against passions, we hold ourselves accountable, repent, humble ourselves and keep fighting, even when we feel defeated. And we move forward. Humility is all we have. For the time of rigorous ascetic races has gone by; possibly irrevocably.

10. Put yourselves in the dock and hold yourselves accountable. Why so? Very simply: your conscience will immediately start talking and if you pay attention, it will tell you a lot. You have no choice but to agree with what it reveals, about any bad deed or

thought. You then turn to God in humility and ask for forgiveness. There were some saints, whose whole life was a constant fight of self-deprecation; a continuous, non-interrupted line. For us of course, this feat is far off. But we too take strength, spiritual strength, when we accuse ourselves. How that happens, we do not know! It is a principle of the spiritual life.

11. What is self-deprecation? It is humility. If you see yourself as guilty and a sinner, it means you have humbled yourself. What is humility? "The divine cloak" says Saint John Climacus. When we reproach ourselves, it is like approaching and kissing that cloak. Remember the bleeding woman in the Gospel? She pushed through the crowd and humbly touched Jesus' cloak; as soon as she did, she was healed! That was all, the Gospel recounts. It was very stark and real. This event also has another more spiritual meaning. It is an analysis of self-deprecation. And so beautiful it is, that I couldn't find a better one in any of the holy fathers, as far as I can remember.

12. Pride is followed by fornication, step by step. It is therefore good to hold ourselves accountable and humble ourselves. Many ascend to heaven carrying with them many great feats and achievements, but they do not wish to humble themselves! That's a problem; the sore of contemporary monasticism. So, be humble!

13. Reject all empty and vain thoughts. Pay no attention to them. A monastic is always at war with such thoughts. Because vanity, when strengthened, becomes full-blown pride. Vanity makes the voiceless

sing, the idle diligent and the coward courageous! The venerable saint John Cassian the Roman was greatly surprised upon noticing this. Surprised at the cunningness, craftiness and evilness of the devil. How the saints avoided vanity! With what great care they dealt with it! Starets Ambrosius always kept a rod by his side. When anyone proceeded to say anything that could awaken vanity, he would pick up the rod and start moving it up and down. Someone once asked: "Elder, why are you doing that?". "Well, because I think it will soon be on your back! So let's stop this conversation here. It's for the best"! While starets Ambrosius was still alive, he would often appear to different people in person (not in their sleep; anything can happen in a dream!), give them advice and save them from danger. When they asked him how he appeared to people in their wake, without leaving his cell, he answered: "It wasn't me, but my angel".

14. Glory is beneficial to no-one. Not to laymen, not even to the saints (e.g. elder father Ambrosius). Because mankind is inclined to evil; and the human heart, though it may belong to a saint, is inclined to glory. The elder Anatolius actually fell ill upon hearing that Saint John of Kronstadt had seen him in a vision, reciting the Liturgy alongside angels! He fasted and prayed! He pleaded with God to take away this thought from his mind! Why? He feared the love of self. He was scared of the thought: "This is what I am"! Because then everything would be lost of course!

15. You should drive away all thoughts and vain aspirations of possibly becoming a starets or an igumen. It is not allowed for us to want those things.

But it may come to happen. May God raise you to that place. However, he might choose to 'bury' you somewhere, in some cell. For the Lord, forgive me! Because I regard myself as ever so slightly above the least of all!

## VI. On reproach and suspicion

1. There is no temptation, when life is hard. As soon as you start to find your bearings, sorrows and trials come your way. This whole fellowship of monks consists of humans. And given they are human, every one of them is being tortured by a passion of some kind. All of us come to the monastery, as though it were a hospital. In order to be healed with God's help. If therefore you see weaknesses in the brothers, don't condemn them. All human beings are weak. We all have passions. And we should all forgive one another.

2. For our whole lifetime, we will be fighting against the passions of annoyance and reproach. When I arrived at the monastery in father Anatolius' time, I said to him:

-I would like to live in as much reclusion as possible.

-Enclosed?

-Yes.

-And you won't bathe?

-Most certainly not.

-Alright, this is my first commandment. You will never bathe again!

-Father, do you mean something else by 'bath'?

-Indeed. Neither solitude nor reclusion can cleanse us. I can still live in the desert with all my passions, if I chose to! And only seemingly not sin. For it is impossible to recognise your weakness and fault in that setting. Here however they "clean" us. Just wait until the back-biting starts! Then hold on tight! Whether you want or not, here they will wash you! That is how we come to understand our weaknesses: annoyance, indignation, reproach, malice, love of self. And we are humbled.

3. Never condemn anyone. Especially for something that "seemed" bad to you. This is a difficult passion. You will find it hard to defeat.

4. Be wary of suspicions. The devil has power over the one who trusts his prompt to be suspicious. He even tells them things, that are non-existent. Whenever Satan shows you other people's weaknesses and ellipses and encourages you towards reproach, tell yourself: "I am worse than everyone. I am worthy of eternal hell. Lord, have mercy". Even if you only say it half-heartedly, you should still say it!

5. In one instance, Nicholas told the Elder that he was having bad thoughts of reproach against him (his elder) regarding his words and teachings; they seemed irrelevant to the monastic way of life. The elder replied:
-When such thoughts come to you, to condemn either the elder or those who mutter to his expense, reply to the thought thus: "This is none of my business, but the elder's. Let him be the one to reply. What place do I have in this?" The elder father Leon gave this answer to a similar question: "My child, we often don't understand, what ordinary people say; or why they say it. Much more do we not understand what

the elders say. We see in the lives of the saints, that even they told jokes. E.g. St Pachomius, St Anthony the Great etc. Obviously they didn't take these jokes from the Holy Scriptures or from the works of the saints. They simply said something "in jest". So do I. I recount something funny, in the very moment satan wanted to depress you. And the joke drove him away."

6. All doubtful, obscene or blasphemous thoughts are to be despised: we should pay them no attention. Despise them. The enemy, the devil will then find it unbearable and leave. The Devil cannot bear being despised, for he is conceited. However, if you start a conversation with these thoughts (remember, those thoughts are not your own, they come from the outside, from the enemy!), the devil will send you so many thoughts that you won't be able to bear the burden; and thus he will "kill" you.
The person who believes in God and loves Him, does not blaspheme. He does notice two trains of thought within him nonetheless: loving and blaspheming. It thus becomes apparent that some evil power from the outside is bringing in the doubts and those obscene and blasphemous thoughts.

Therefore, despise those thoughts. Only then will they not harm you! Especially if you reveal them to the elder. While you are telling him, do not go into detail, for it is possible to harm both yourself and the elder. You should especially make sure you don't recount details of adulterous thoughts. It is best, if you completely close and cover that dirty cesspit. Don't mess around with it. Those immoral and impure thoughts will only be counted to you as sin, if you start to take pleasure in them.

Only the saints can drive these thoughts away by refuting them. The rest of us can be saved only by running away. Whenever you do not have the strength to fight and triumph over impure thoughts, call upon the Lord; and then His name will drive them away.

Unconfessed sin has a drastic effect on the soul and leads it to death.

7. We have gone down the wrong route, if we think all problems can be solved in a purely intellectual manner; when trying to sort out doubts and unsolvable issues (dead ends). The enemy confuses us completely. The longer a monk lives in the monastery, the more he will learn, the wiser he will become. It happens gradually. Only God can enlighten people's minds, so that they come to know the truth. Intelligence and discernment are two distinct things. Both of them are a gift from God. But discernment is the highest gift, not granted easily! Someone may be very clever but lack the gift of discernment. Sensual people live only for their stomach and sexual immorality. Others, who are more intellectual and somewhat connected with their soul, are in a slightly better state. Then there are spiritual people. They are very different to the previous category. Somewhat aware people still do not accept what is of the spirit; they think it is nonsense. They can attain all human wisdom and still lack spiritual discernment. "For the word of the cross is folly to those who are perishing, but to us who are being saved it is the power of God". And did you notice

what he said: “those who are being saved”, not “those who were saved”; and “those who are perishing” not “those who have perished”. Many readers don’t even pay attention to these details. We are the ones “who are being saved”; ie those striving to be saved, but unsure if we will be saved in the end. And the others are called “those who are perishing”, not already perished, because it is still possible for them to repent, even though they are completely in a state ‘of the flesh’, sinking deeper into the mud.

8. When reading books, do not lose yourself in the detail; don’t get carried away by over analysing, but instead pray; ask God to enlighten your mind. When I once asked starets Anatolius “why?”, he replied: “You will get confused”. In the books of the Holy Scriptures and the holy Fathers there are passages that are confusing and create questions; e.g. demons, the heavenly altar, angelic hosts etc. All these should be understood in a spiritual sense. They allude to a different reality, unknown to us, one we cannot attain and that cannot be expressed in human words. Some of course are scandalised, because they do not understand, that these words should not be understood in their literal, word-for-word sense but somehow differently; spiritually.

9. On a daily basis, every night, search yourselves and repent of your sins. Keeping our life in checkmates us aware of our weakness and leads us to repentance; and repentance leads us to a continuous remembrance of God and death. I discern in you the start of a wise and self-controlled life. Idle chatter hinders ablution, for it makes us constantly scatter-brained. Silence brings forth peace. Peace produces prayer. Is it

possible for man to pray, when his thoughts are all over the place? Take care. A life of cleansing and awareness facilitates prayer and brings us close to God. “Take care of yourself”. Silence is to be exercised. The one who practices it, should expect sorrows, given silence is acquired slowly and painfully. However, it is such a high and noble virtue for salvation, that “silence is the mystery of the future age to come”. By being silent, you prepare yourself for the future life. The elder Macarius often told us these words.

10. The fear of the world and of a worldly life is a salutary fear. Escape from this awful beast, the world. May God grant that you escape from him completely. Be fearful of sin. We see in the holy Bible, that God does not love cowards. It is therefore unfitting for a monk to be timid and cowardly. He should put his hope in God. God does not love cowards, for they are so close to despairing! And disappointment, despair is a deadly sin. A true monk should be a complete stranger to this psychological state.

11. It is wrong for us to become angry towards those who cause us grief. They are our best benefactors. They reveal our imperfections, which we may have never realised on our own! So we should treat them calmly and pray for them. A calm reaction can prove miraculous. How was the tax collector saved? By one thing alone: the recognition of his sinfulness. “God, be merciful to me, a sinner”. This prayer is 2.000 years old. But notice this: the tax collector is completely aware that he is a sinner and at the same time he is asking for God’s mercy. Salvation is impossible without hope. The Lord said: I did not

come to save “the righteous”, but sinners. Who do we mean by “the righteous”? It is obvious that he is also talking about sinners, who are unconscious of their sinfulness; and of demons. We cannot even fathom the pride, with which they stand before God. It is impossible for us to understand, how much they hate God. And God opposes the proud; but to the humble he gives grace. Why does the Bible not say that God dislikes the sexually impure or other sinners, but instead the proud? Because pride is a quality that demons have. Because in some way, a proud person is the devil’s relative.

Someone told his Elder:
- I read the psalter, but I did not understand a thing. I suppose then, that it would be best for me, if I left this book to the side.

The elder answered him:
- No. You shouldn’t.

-Why so? For I understand nothing.

-Maybe you do not understand; but the demons understand, that it’s talking about them; and they cannot bear it and will leave.

12. Some sins are deadly; other sins are not deadly. A sin is deadly, when man does not repent of it. It is called deadly, because it kills the soul; and after the physical death it goes to hades. Only through repentance can a soul live again! A deadly sin kills the soul; it renders it incapable of spiritual life. Take a blind person. Place them in a spot with a wonderful view and tell them: “What a beautiful view”! What

will their reply be? What else? “I cannot see a thing; I am blind”! The same thing happens to the soul, that has been made dead by sin and is unable to see eternal bliss.

13. Music is an art. There is also such a thing as music of the soul. It’s internal peace. The Gospel says of this peace: “Take my yoke upon you; and learn from me, for I am gentle and lowly in heart, and you will find rest for your souls; for my yoke is easy and my burden is light.” That is what peace and rest look like. If you studied math, you know the symbol, that stands for “equal” (=). Well, there you have it! It is the internal peace of the soul. It’s blessedness; music; harmony; a harmony of all the soul’s attributes and strengths.

14. Beyond its very obvious meaning, everything in the gospel, has another further meaning, a more mystical, more cryptic one.

15. Maybe later on you will become a spiritual father. I warn you now. Guard yourself from women. You should be as careful as you can. You cannot imagine how complicated the human soul is. Praise God, that you didn’t get married! I warn you therefore. Be careful. They create a havoc for no reason! Spiritual daughters and nuns fall in the same category. Be as careful as you can. They complain to me about father Joseph and about me to father Joseph! One time, father Joseph’s helper said to me:
“Elder, don’t believe them! They lie constantly! They do the same thing at their monastery. They go from cell to cell causing a stir! And not occasionally; all the time!” In an attempt to describe the situation, I

have come up with a slogan: “A nun will hold on to all the ‘back and forth’, until she gets onto the monastic path properly”! She stops only once she acquires the monastic mentality. Some acquire it in a year's time, others in two. Some in five or ten and some in twenty years. Whichever of them has some predisposition to the monastic mentality, gets onto this path fairly quickly. Others though do not get on the right track at all! They came, they saw, they left! However, there are also nuns who have very deep spiritual thoughts.

16. A woman does not live without faith. Disbelief in a woman is temporary. She will always return to faith, to God. Otherwise she quickly falls apart. Men are a different story. He can live without faith. He becomes a rock, a whitewashed wall, a pillar of salt. But even so, he can keep on going.

17. The Gospel, and the holy Scriptures in general, are full of mysteries. That’s where depth is to be found. A depth of unfathomable meanings. It’s impossible to understand everything. As with an onion, you first peel one layer, then the next, then the third one, and so on. The same thing happens, when studying the Scriptures. We understand the meaning and straight away we realise there is also another deeper, hidden meaning. This hidden, mystical meaning is revealed to us, according to how much we cleanse our minds. To one more, to another less. But even a little bit is adequate for life. Thus God enlightens the minds of His athletes.

18. Education is not a hindrance, in fact it facilitates spiritual progress.

19. The prophet David says: “The Lord is my strength and my song”. “ I will sing to the Lord”. “I will sing praise to my God as long as I live”. This praise to the Lord happens non-verbally. To acquire it, we go to the monasteries. That’s where we get it. Some obtain it in five years. Others in forty. May God grant that you also may receive this gift. And if anything, be joyful, because you are on the way that leads to it. In the Holy Bible we read of “islands”. “In God the islands will put their hope”. How do islands hope in God? Monasteries are referred to as islands. And the whole passage informs us that when the antichrist comes, faith may very well be preserved only in monasteries!

20. The starets (elder) Macarius once told his successor, father Anatolius:
-We have an obligation to go to church, before the service begins.

-Why?

-I will tell you some other time.

And a few years later he said:
-Because that is when Panagia comes to the Temple.

21. We cannot comprehend the hidden meaning of life-happenings by our own power. It’s a gift from above. However, if you stay on this path, you will be able to delve into the meaning of events, only with Jesus’ prayer. Then you will see greater things than these, just as Jesus told Nathanael. When you starts to see what you couldn’t make out at first and people

around you still cannot see, that's when you know the cleansing of the mind has started.

22. Indescribable torment awaits sinners in hades. And indescribable blessedness awaits the righteous. "No eye has seen and no ear has heard". These words of the apostle fit well with both the torment and the blessedness. We sometimes think of punishment in hades very abstractly. And that's why we forget about it. The world doesn't even concede to its existence! The devil implants in people the thought that there is no devil, no hell, no hades. And yet the holy fathers tell us, that on earth you get a for-taste of hell, as you do of eternal blessing. Sinners begin to feel the punishment of hades, and the righteous start to feel joy. There is a crucial difference though: both the punishment and the joy will be far greater in the future life. Indisputably so. Hell exists. And it will come to pass! At that time the souls of both righteous and sinners will be clothed, no longer with this heavy body but a lighter and more ethereal one. This will all come about before Judgement takes place. After Judgement Day, no-one knows what will happen. Not even the angels. It's God's secret. Everything the Church teaches is true. And after death there is torment. According to the holy Fathers, judgment will take place at midnight. It will come upon all the inhabitants of earth suddenly and without warning. Like a thief!

23. We will not enter paradise through our own labour and good works, but because of the grace and value of the redeeming sacrifice of our God and Saviour Jesus Christ. Our good works, our obedience to the Gospel's commandments are only a testimony

of our love for Christ. Without love for the Lord, blessings and paradise cannot be attained.

24. For a long time I could not understand the words of the psalm: “The voice of the Lord flashes forth flames of fire” (Psalm 28,7). I was pondering: an earthly flame consists both of fire and light. So between hades and paradise, the flame is distributed as follows: the light is in paradise; it makes the righteous rejoice. The fire, without any light, is in hell; it consumes the sinners. The Bible says: the flame’s abyss in hades is darkness. Sinners do not see one another! Lord, save us and have mercy on us. Discipline me, as you please. Only have mercy on me, Lord.

25. The horrors of hell and hades are constantly on my mind, though I speak of them to no-one and my countenance does not give me away. I use this feeling of horror to keep myself humble; and it really does! The wise of our age do not admit hell exists! Let us rise and pray that the Lord may exempt us from the fiery furnace of hell. Let us also thank Him that we are here. May our whole life be a thanksgiving offering, for the fact that the Lord led us to this place. Obviously the place alone does not save us. But at least we know we are in a lifeboat. These new inventions end up causing more harm than good, even though they aim to benefit us. We will witness terrible times! But God’s grace will cover us!

26. Christianity is now hated everywhere! It’s a burden to them! It gets in the way of them living, as they please! Of committing sins freely! The new generation is falling apart, it’s perishing and rotting.

They want to live without God. And there you have it: The result is obvious!

27. The whole world is under the influence of a force, that controls the mind, will and willpower of the soul. That force is evil. Its source is the devil. Evil people are only the instruments through which he works. He is the antichrist, who is coming. And his forerunners. This is why the apostle says: “God sends them a strong delusion, so that they may believe what is false, because they refused to love the truth”. Something dark and horrendous is coming into the world. Mankind will be more or less defenceless and have no awareness of its actions, for the time it is under the power of the evil one.

28. At present we do not have live sources-prophecies within our Church; we do have signs though; in order to understand the signs the times. These signs are clear only to those who have Christ’s mind. It is now crystal clear. The antichrist is coming into the world. Yet the world does not accept this statement as true. From here, from the monastery, the devil’s nets can be seen much more clearly. Eyes are opened here! In the world they are closed. Be thankful to the Lord that you left the world behind.

29. It is worth noting that unbelievers, materialists, do not move past what is visible. They reject the existence not only of angels and demons but of God himself. And when hell is mentioned, they completely refuse to accept that it can be perceived by the senses! This contradiction has been noticed by a lot of great men.

30. You may already know, that where churches, monasteries and other holy places stand today, there used to be idols and idolatrous temples. We often read in the lives of the saints: "And where there used to be a temple, a Church was founded", ie what God wanted, so that the devil would be shamed. But in the last days, churches will be demolished and idolatrous shrines will be built in their place. Monasteries will suffer brutal persecution and afflictions. True Christians will find refuge in tiny churches! May I not still be alive at that time! But you will be. You will be at the monasteries that suffer from persecution and deprivation! I will be buried in the cold, wet ground by that point! And my spiritual daughter will come to my grave and tell me: "Father Barsanuphius, please help me; intercede for me. I am in a very difficult situation"! Yes, my daughter. This is what will come to pass!

31. We read in Revelation: "Blessed is the reader of the words of this book". If it says so, then it will surely be so. For the words of Scripture are words of the Holy Spirit. What then is this blessedness? The more some people do not understand what the Bible says, the more they are disappointed. Especially since they know that studying the holy words brings consolation. However, they would be better off if they said: "What we do not understand at present, we will understand at a later date, when the appointed time comes". Tell me. Where is the Apocalypse read nowadays? Almost exclusively in monasteries, theological colleges and seminaries. Rarely in the rest of the world. No-one reads it. When the end of the world is here, whoever has been reading Revelation will be truly blessed; because they will be able to

understand some of what is happening at that time. And they will start to prepare themselves. They will see all the events described in Revelation, come alive before their eyes.

32. The starets took a Bible and opened to III Ezra and pointing to a passage, underlined in blue ink, said: “Read this”. The age is no longer young, and the times are beginning to grow old. The age is divided into twelve parts. Nine parts and half of the tenth have already passed (III Ezra 14,10-12).
This book is full of mysteries. Many have attempted the calculations; in all of them the twentieth century is when the end comes, our times. And actually there are a lot of signs. We are departing; you will be the ones to live through and endure all those big events. For you will still be alive, when they come.

33. In every single ecclesiastical institution there is great depth to be found! For example, why do we have the grave sound (the Seventh) during Trinity week? That’s because number 7 is sacred. On the seventh day the Lord rested after creating the world. The sacraments are seven. Seven are the gifts of the Holy Spirit. And so on. Next we have All Saints week, with the plagal of the Fourth sound, ie the Eighth. Why? Because number 8 symbolises infinity; in other words the future age. Saints leave this world awaiting the future and their rebirth. They attained holiness on earth! Is it ever possible that they would change now? That they would falter? That they would slacken in their love for God? No. They will keep being perfected in their love forever.

34. It is likely that the persecution and tortures of first Christians will be repeated! All these things are possible nowadays. Hades has been crushed but not completely obliterated. And there will come a time, where we will get to very good grips with that fact. The monasteries will be destroyed! And Christians who hold an office will be dismissed! That time isn't far off. Remember my words. You will still be alive, when those times come to be! Then you will say: "I remember! This is what father Barsanuphius was telling us about". How many years have gone by. There will come a time, when Optina will go through difficult days! Maybe it's for the better.

35. The 43rd catechism of the venerable Saint Theodore the Studite, read on the Sunday of Orthodoxy, is perfectly contemporary, even though it was written a thousand years ago. And the Lord willing, another thousand years will go by and it will keep being read! And it will never lose its value.

36. You will live to see the day, when they start torturing Christians again.

-They are being tortured at present as well; though not as fiercely.

-No. I am not talking about that sort of torture. I am referring to tortures identical to the ancient ones!

37. Religiousness is passed on hereditarily. From Cain comes forth an ungodly generation; from Abel a generation faithful to God. For heredity in a spiritual relationship functions quite like physical heredity.

38. Awful things were recounted to me about a monk. What is to happen when Optina is full of such monks? Obviously I won't be alive, when that happens! But you will have a great struggle ahead of you! You will have to pour out plenty of sweat and blood and tears. The Lord will not allow it. Optina will continue to exist!

39. Keep this in mind; in 1925 it will be exactly a hundred years since the Skete was founded!

40. The fifth volume of Bishop Ignatius includes a lot of the fathers' teachings regarding contemporary monasticism. It teaches us how to read the patristic books. Bishop Ignatius was profoundly insightful when it came to this; even more that Bishop Theophan the Recluse. His words affect the soul in a very powerful way, because they are the fruit of his personal experience. He was a great mind! You know what happened at Bishop Ignatius' burial. Angels surrounded his soul as it ascended to Heaven, in great glory. And they sang: "Archpriest of God, Hierarch father Ignatius, mediate and hail". What an angelic song!

## VII. On Elders

1. Elder Ambrosius didn't have any particularly close disciples, apart from father Anatolius, who was literally his "co-initiate". Elder Ambrosius had no enemies. He loved everyone, even those who didn't love him. And there were a few of those. Even nowadays there are monks in our monastery who want to hear nothing of father Ambrosius! "A prophet

is not without honour, except in his hometown”! Russia honours the venerable Seraphim as a nation. And yet he was hated in his monastery! Indeed. “A prophet is not without honour, except in his hometown”.

2. Elder Leon endured a great number of persecution from seemingly well-wishers. Even Nicholas the bishop of Kaluga, upon seeing him surrounded by people, told him angrily: “what are you doing there?”. He replied: “I sing praises unto my God, for as long as I exist”. The despot understood the deeper meaning of those words. Starets Leon indeed sang to the Lord with all his strength throughout his lifetime.

3. The Elder Ambrosius has said:
-Agitation is not numbered amongst the virtues; for the one behind it is the Liar and Father of Lies.
-Faith should be ever-present in the relation of disciple and elder. Consequently, the Lord acts according to the faith of the inquirer; and in His compassion, He reveals His will to the Elder.
-The enemy gets very jealous, when he sees us communicating with each other honestly and lovingly in the Lord. He then attempts to sow enmity and discord; because he hates good. Therefore I say to you: The enemy will not leave without attacking honest and genuine relationships, that resemble the relationship of a father and his children. On a number of occasions he has succeeded in separating saints! But I’m telling you: If we endeavour to always cultivate simplicity and honesty with one another, even if we reveal our thoughts, he will not be able to harm us. Our diligence in revealing our thoughts to one another, will dissolve his evil.

4. I understand now how an elder and his disciple used to live in olden times. They lived as though they shared one soul. I speak to you now, just like an elder would speak to his disciple then.

## VIII. On trials and tribulations

1. Everyone must go through a period of sorrow and tribulations and war. It's a painful and difficult experience, "Anguish as of a woman in labour" (Psalm 47,6). Every man or woman, when spiritually born to new life, experiences pain; but as time goes on, they gradually move towards joy. Whoever didn't go through this "anguish as of a woman in labour" in the world, will experience it in the monastery. The same goes for you. These pains of childbirth are the fight against passions. Passions will revolt. The enemy will not give up on fighting you. This is where patience is required. You will have to endure your very selves. And don't you quit! Know this: passions are inevitable.

2. God-sent tribulations that hit us like wave after wave, are a sign of God's love for us. The aim of each differs. God sends them our way to stop us from doing something bad or to discipline us; or to glorify us even more in the future life; or to punish us for older sins. Everyone carries their cross. You must bear yours also! Carry it! Even if just with your little finger! Bear it. It's essential for everyone's salvation; not just for monastics. Yes, they all took or take up a cross. The incarnate God himself carried His own Cross. And His Cross was the heaviest; because it

contained all of our crosses. Yet someone (Simon of Cyrene) helped Him. He took up the Christ's Cross and carried it himself. As we carry our own crosses, we also should help our Lord by preparing ourselves to become His ministers in heaven, to be numbered amongst the multitude of bodiless spirits. What a grand destination!

3. "Put not your trust in princes, in a son of man, in whom there is no salvation.". I have always loved studying the Bible and the works of the holy Fathers. Especially the Psalter. What depths of wisdom have been revealed to me! Put your hope in God alone. Never in man; if you do, every type of evil will fall upon you, like branches snapped off a tree.

4. The more diligently and frugally you live, the more viciously the enemy will attack you. He mainly endeavours to drag you into sin during times of celebration. Anything could happen. Be alert. The Lord is compassionate. Gifts are given on festive days. You also will receive something. You may realise after a number of years; maybe even 40 years. Then you will realise, what gift the Lord sent you that one holiday.

5. Whenever you are in a good state of mind, expect a storm. That's what always happens. Temptation either precedes or succeeds anything good!

6. When you are encountering a great number of sorrows, tell yourself this: "Maybe I am worthy of these tribulations. Maybe they are all necessary for me to be cleansed of my passions, pride in particular." It is no tremendous feat to endure various

hardships. We should prioritise not ending up filled with bitterness towards the one who caused them.

7. We shall always have sorrows. But our internal state should be different. The one who has attained internal prayer will endure sorrows easily, no matter their number, because Christ will be with him. They will be filled with unspeakable joy. And no sorrow can destroy that joy, joy in the Lord.

8. When you are agitated by thoughts of fear about future tribulations, do not start a conversation with them. Simply say: "May the will of the Lord be done". You will be filled with peace.

9. In my morning prayers, I utter the wretched words: "oh Lord, have mercy on me, a sinner", so that I may not be called to answer for my silence on Judgment Day.

10. Brother Nicholas, though it is not the first time, I will say it again: I often have this thought of just leaving everything behind and enclosing myself in a cell. It is a terrifying thing for one to live, my brother Nicholas! Terrifying! Only I am afraid to go on my own. And I have no-one I can ask for advice. Now I start to understand the meaning of the prophet David's words: "Save me, oh Lord". If we take this phrase on it own, we see that no-one wants to be lost forever. Everyone is very willing to say "Save me, oh Lord". But David adds to that phrase: "for the godly one is gone". That is, I have no man to turn to! Save me, oh Lord! Now I get why the holy Fathers left for the desert. No-one can go there completely on their own. But they can, when God is with them. For

example, the bishop Theophan the Recluse tried to leave everything and go into isolation on multiple occasions. But it wasn't the will of God. When he had started to miss it, an answer from God came in the form of a transfer to the archdiocese of Vladimir. After a few years though he withdrew to his beloved Vissa. When will we go to our Vissa, brother Nicholas? Soon? Later? In any case, we should definitely go! Yes, my brother, we should. The thought of coveted reclusion never leaves me! But for now it is impossible. I am scared. "Why did you leave your sentry box?" the Lord will ask me. I have the duty to endure. For if I leave my post, the souls ordained by God to be saved through me, might not be saved!

11. In my lifetime I have noticed that dead ends and incomprehensible situations get enlightened on their own accord, sometimes fairly quickly, sometimes years later. That's why I have never insisted on explaining them, because I believed that someday they would be revealed to me. Indeed, the Lord would answer my questions at the right time.

12. Always be a small child with regards to malice; not intellectually. When it comes to your mind, be perfect men. Stand firm and immovable in your places. You are on the right path. You left the world and all its noise. You didn't hide your talent in the soil. I am saying this to strengthen and encourage you. The ones who bury their talent in the soil, are those who leave the post they were assigned to, according to God's will. The venerable Seraphim of Sarov resigned from his post as dignitary. How he suffered for that! He nearly fell into despair! And it

was necessary to take on that great feat, of staying on the rock for three years, in order to defeat those temptations! That is what it means to leave one’s place. An archimandrite once asked me: “If you resign and leave, will you be able to bear what will happen to you?” Behold, this is why I remain in my place.

13. Sometimes I have thoughts that the monastic life is a bleak and joyless life. The days go by monotonously and there is nothing to look forward to! The Elder replied: “This is the most poisonous thought”! A monk should always feel “birth pains”, in order to reach perfect manhood and maturity. But as long as the old self lives within us, he will keep reminding us of his presence through our passions: the boredom and disappointment we feel. Whatever feels most burdensome for the old self, will later be our greatest consolation. At that time, everything will be filled with light and joy in the Lord. Then will be fulfilled the words of the psalm: “I was glad when they said to me, let us go to the house of the Lord”. When this thought agitates you, say: “Do not worry about what will happen! The Lord will help me tread this path. I do not suppose I will reach the highest ranks of perfection; but I hope to be saved”!

14. The secret of spiritual strength lies in self-denial. Self-denial for the sake of our Lord Jesus Christ. Denial of everything, whatever it may be. Regard everything as rubbish, for the Lord's sake. It’s an important facet of the spiritual life. In order to progress spiritually, e.g. Christ’s prayer, all sorts of sorrows, bitterness and humiliations are necessary; particularly slander. I wish to warn you of the sorrows

that await you from demons, humans and the scandals of this world. You must endure all. Only thus will you enter the joy and bliss of Christian love and freedom from passions.

15. Seek to follow in the example of the saint who's name you bear, regarding thoughts and deeds. Saint Nicholas was renowned for his zeal, his orthodox faith and his love for God and mankind.

16. Confession and recounting our thoughts to someone, they are not the same thing. The holy fathers say: When I have no-one to turn to for confession, I may chose a like-minded brother and tell them my thoughts. In other words: We can recount our thoughts to someone who is not a priest (for advice); but not confess our sins, for them to grant us remission!

17. Our mind is a self-motored power, but what direction we'll guide it in, that is up to us. Just like the millstone that goes round and round, but it's up to the person using it to decide what they will grind: wheat, barley or other poisonous seeds. The same goes for the mind.

## IX. The Jesus Prayer

(lyrics by starets Barsanuphius, free verse translation)

1. It all starts on the narrow way.
It will never linger in a busy soul.
Affliction and mockery,
sickness, contempt and toil
attack the warrior

on all sides;
and there he stands agitated,
full of dark thoughts and wonder.
His soul is full to the brim
with weariness and fatigue!
But no! Prayer
will scatter his enemies,
one and all.

2. If your aim is
to set humility before God as the roof above your head,
for it is God's cloak,
never will you give
the invisible enemies of your salvation
the joy of your defeat.
Endure every attack in your mind
with patience;
and never consider
forsaking the narrow and sorrowful way;
For that is your only guarantee
of God's promised gifts.

3. Live for eternity,
the only true and indestructible beauty;
And forget what is fake and just a dream.
Contend like a man in this hard race
and you will be filled with a life full of light;
and the hour will strike, the time will come,
the inner struggle will cease,
that painful price of our love for passions.
Then with joy and ease
you shall be rid of your burden,
tribulations, bitterness, temptations.
Your soul shall not disturb

the constant dizziness of dubious thoughts.
No, your soul shall bask in the never-setting light of the Saviour.
And in you will come to dwell
the peace of God that transcends all understanding;
and you shall become the heir
of heaven's wonders.
While in this life, your soul shall be
the Garden of Eden.
For it will be in perfect unison
with our God, Saviour and Lord, Jesus Christ.
Then shall vanish every pain, sorrow and groan
leaving no trace behind them.
And -surprising though it may be- you shall find within you
the dawning of a great and shining New Earth.

4. He became a stranger to joy and peace;
and he has no hope in anyone
but Christ alone.
Yet his spiteful enemies scream at him from all around:
Woe! Woe unto you!
If He is God, let Him come down from the Cross for you!

5. My brother in Christ,
endure with courage!
never stop fighting the big fight,
not even for a second.
Don't retreat from the battleground in fear,
don't leave; never give up on prayer.
Persevere in this "work" until the end;
until your end.
Victory is there for you, oh warrior.

Don’t let your body weigh you down.
Don’t allow difficulties and obstacles to get in the way.
When like insidious and deceitful visitors
come the innumerable multitudes
of twisted thoughts,
you shall prevail in the almighty Name
of Jesus Christ.

**Miscellaneous**

1. A love of vanity smothers faith in the heart.

2. Even when monasteries cease to exist, our monastic promises are not annulled, because we gave them before the Lord. Our monastic identity remains intact whatever the circumstances. In the past. The present. And the future.

3. The portion and lot of those who wish to be saved is pain. We should rejoice, when we suffer, because it's a safer way of treading the road to salvation.

4. As a human being, I am a big fat zero. Yet I am a priest. And by the grace of Priesthood I can do everything, that priesthood grants me the right to accomplish.

5. Everything I have done and still do, I do by the grace of Priesthood. I received priesthood freely. Firstly, because from a material point of view, there is nothing that can buy it. Secondly, because from an ethical point of view, I was not worthy to receive such a great gift. When I think of it, I am filled with fear. And I humbly ask God to help me to use this priesthood according to His holy will.

6. I am very sinful. Yet I am a monk. In other words: I am certainly a man of God and I have completely surrendered myself to his care.

7. We should always keep the spirit of our age in consideration. We should never allow ourselves to be carried away by our older perceptions, which no longer resonate with the present. We must never forget that our Christian identity -not our monastic identity- is what matters for us and is truly valuable. Monasticism is just the methodical approach to perfection in the Christian life.

8. Never bother yourself with the opinions of people, who have no ecclesiastical mindset.

9. When you come into Church, keep in mind that the Church is the House of God. And stand there, continuously aware that you are in God's House. Keep in mind every single second that God is right there, next to you. And never ever allow yourself any freedom or carelessness of movement for the time you find yourself in Church.

10. Continuous prayer is a gift from God.

11. Forgiveness is granted to us only when we deem ourselves accountable, guilty and responsible for our actions. Therefore, humble yourself before God and before people. Then, God will never leave you nor forsake you.

12. God's peace in our hearts comes from a sincere desire to keep God's will. So give yourself over to the holy will of God wholeheartedly, a will so good and perfect, and God will give you peace, even as you endure a lot of internal and external hardships. Always put yourself, everything and everyone into God's hands.

13. Plead with God for him to remove any tribulation. At the same time, renounce your own sinful and blind will. Give yourself, your soul, your body, your possessions, your present and your future, your acquaintances, your friends, your family, everything - give them over to the ever-holy and ever-wise will of God. Say: Praise be to You, o God. Praise be to You, o God. Praise be to You, o God. For everything. All dark thoughts dissolve with these wonderful and holy words, and the heaviness is lifted from one's soul, and in come peace, consolation, joy. Your will be done, Lord. In everything. Praise be to You, Lord. For everything.

14. We must never give in to disappointment. Let's not forget that God's infinite compassion is hidden even in our hardest experiences. In inconceivable ways (and often unacceptable in our eyes!) God builds us up. Even the loss of a spiritual father is part of God's holy plans for our salvation. Trust me.

15. Life ends up being intolerable, when there is no patience or consideration towards our neighbour.

16. Physical separation does not dissolve the spiritual bond between two people. It doesn't negate love in the Lord, which is the most precious thing on earth.

17. Trust me: when you persevere through very difficult situations, you are persevering according to and in God's will. For your salvation.

18. It is always possible that humans will err in their judgement. At that point, their judgement becomes

nothing more than idle talk. Only the Lord sees the human heart.

19. All our good works must be tried; that is, they must be tested for authenticity before God. All of them. Even our faith. This trial will come with bitterness and pain.

20. Sometimes God lets humans feel like he has rejected and forgotten them. That can happen not only on an individual but also a collective level; society on the whole. In those situations, our job is to preserve faith in Christ. If the faith is preserved, there is hope of salvation. Faith is protected thus: by abstinence to all sin.

21. If there is no person to open your heart to, tell God about your woes.

22. We should not attach ourselves to earthly matters, precious as they may seem. Appoint an earthly value to every earthly matter. Only one thing is of true value; the salvation of our soul. Everything else is vain. Every single thing on earth is fickle. Our mind should be set on God, our gaze fixed on Him and eternal life. All earthly things will come to pass.

**What is at fault**

**Epilogue**

No-one and nothing can cause man more harm, than the harm one causes to themselves.

To him who does not shun sin, though he may be given a thousand means of salvation and a thousand opportunities, they will be of no avail.

One evil exists in the world: sin.

Judas fell, even though he was constantly by the Saviour's side.

And the righteous Lot was saved, even though he lived in Sodom.

These and other similar thoughts cross my mind, when I study the words of the holy Fathers and take a look at everything happening around us.

(Starets Nikona, letter to his mother)

www.ingramcontent.com/pod-product-compliance
Ingram Content Group UK Ltd.
Pitfield, Milton Keynes, MK11 3LW, UK
UKHW021934190726
13853UKWH00004B/1444